CW01432518

Adverse Childhood Experiences:
Using Constellation Therapy to help repair the damage

Rafe Nauen

Copyright © 2019
Rafe L Nauen

All rights reserved. This book or any portion thereof may not be reproduced or used in any manner whatsoever without the express written permission of the publisher except for the use of brief quotations in a book review.

Printed in the United States of America and Europe

First Printing, 2019

Second printing, 2019

ISBN 978 1790101337

Rafe Nauen
3 Mayfield Road
DERBY
DE21 6FX
UK
http://books.rafenauen.com
rafe@rafenauen.com
+447889 523164

Contents

Dedication

I wish to make life a little better for anyone who happens upon this book, and to provide hope that some of the risks following on from high score ACEs can be reduced. It is never too late to begin the repair work of early life damage, and sometimes you can find unexpected gifts hidden within.

Acknowledgements

Family – my family of origin, and the three systems of family that I have been part of during my life thus far; Thursday group (a group of profoundly enlightened people who have helped me more than they will ever know – Lou Radford, Andrea Spencer, Sarah Hobby and my extraordinary wife Julie Bowman who works with Limbic Reflexology and Flower Essences, Nadine Burke Harris, Isaac Pizer, Richard Wallstein. The clients who have taught me so much and have made this book both needed and possible.

Introduction

I am aware of a vast amount of research in to ACEs (Adverse Childhood Experience) – a subject which includes neglect, starvation, mental physical or sexual abuse (including psychosexual trauma) – The Bibliography at the end of the book lists my sources, but there are many more available – a google search for ACEs yields 1.3 billion results.

I am a counsellor, constellation facilitator, a life coach, a son, a husband, a father, a brother and a grandfather and I have a wide range of experience of life. I am 68 at this time, and many of my clients come to me to explore their situation in a safe space. I have come to know that the safer the space, the deeper the exploration can go.

The Adverse Childhood Experiences Study (ACE Study) is a research study conducted by the American health maintenance organization Kaiser Permanente and the Centre for Disease Control and Prevention. Participants were recruited to the study between 1995 and 1997 and have been in long-term follow up for health outcomes. The study has demonstrated an association of adverse childhood experiences (ACEs) (aka childhood trauma) with health and social problems across the lifespan. The study has produced many scientific articles. There have been conference and workshop presentations that examine ACEs. (Source Wikipedia). The cohort for the original study was 17,000 and the demographic was 70% Caucasian and college educated. The studies reveal the stereotype response to the idea of an alcoholic being attributed to a dirty homeless man drinking from a bottle inside a paper bag. The reality is that that alcoholic could just as easily be a successful businessman or woman, a doctor even, driving a Rolls Royce and drinking a bottle of vodka a day. I have met such people – functioning alcoholics.

Can you repair the damage done by high scores of ACEs? The short answer is "yes", and this book gives some of the information about one major method and references some others.

This book is written to bring together some serious scientific research, some ideas, some experience, and some suggestions. It is written for practitioners who need to understand ACEs better, and for people who suffer from high ACE's scores and wish to understand what they might be able to do about that in order to have A) a better quality of life, and B) to statistically improve the likely quantity and quality of life! (it's been shown that high ACEs scores can triple the likelihood of cancer, diabetes and heart disease.

So, what is an ACEs score? See the list in the Appendices but suffice it to say that there are three categories: Abuse – physical, mental and sexual; Neglect – hungry, unloved or abandonment; Witness – others in family being in other categories, and unable to create safety for them. Inability to find safe space at home. The disturbing feature is that the simple NUMBER of ACEs experienced as a child corelates precisely (straight line graph) to health and wellbeing outcomes in later life – high number ACEs – high risk, low number low risk. This book is designed to help you reduce the risks from high ACEs.

To explain the way ACEs affect us, it is important at the outset to understand what happens in the developing brain that affects health later on.

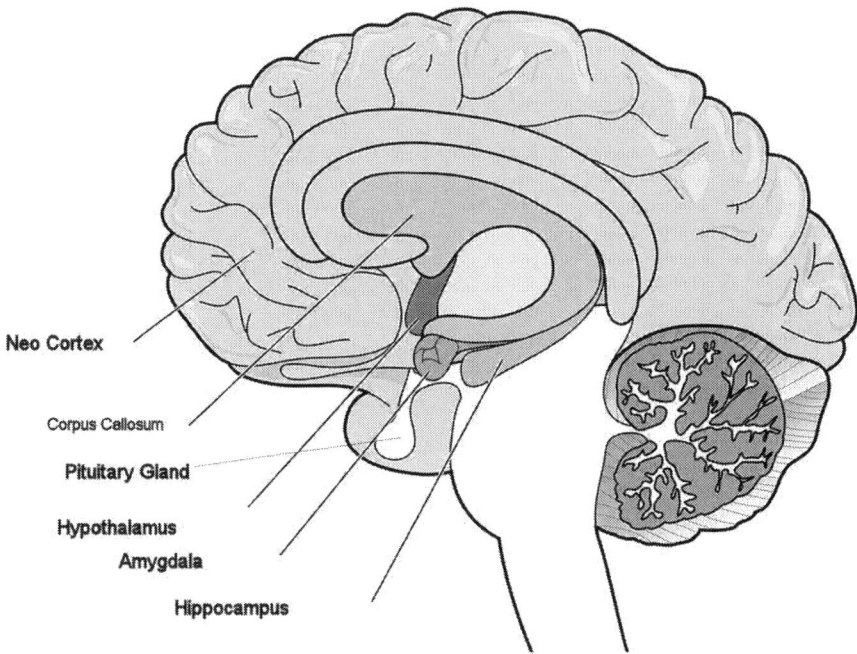

Neo Cortex

Corpus Callosum

Pituitary Gland

Hypothalamus

Amygdala

Hippocampus

The older portions of the brain (the primordial stuff) is the amygdala, hypothalamus and hippocampus. These are used to prepare the primitive human for action when threatened – to keep you safe when danger is around. The later developments are the neo cortex and the corpus callosum. The neo cortex is the rational part, the place of ethics, decisions, greater good concepts etc, and develop in the human later. Clearly a baby needs only to cry to get attention for food, health and love. It does not need reasoning skills until much later.

The two sides the brain control different aspects of humanity – the left being about logic, science maths, controls etc. The right side is about creativity and more artistic stuff – appreciation of beauty. The corpus callosum is a thick band of nerves that control the flow of information between the two hemispheres. In a study published in Science Daily it was shown that a significant proportion of psychopaths had an abnormal corpus callosum affecting the flow of information between the two sides of the hippocampus, thus removing feelings of guilt when perpetrating acts that non-psychopaths would be restricted from doing by their own systemic controls in a well developed neo-cortex.

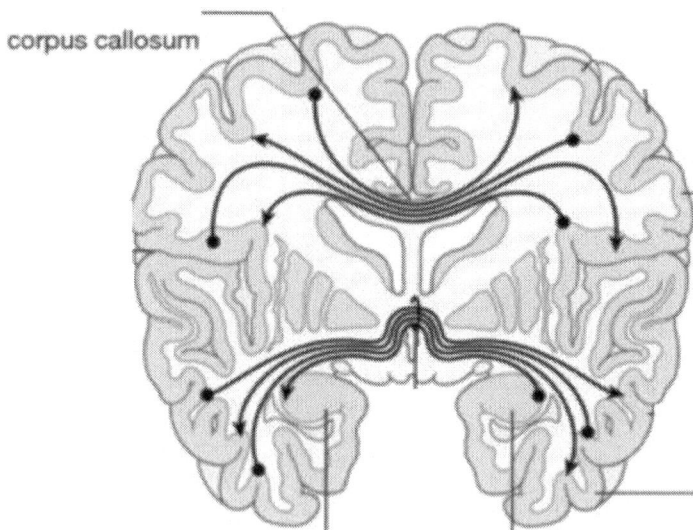

corpus callosum

Briefly:

Say you are in the woods, and you see a bear – several instant things happen:

1. The hypothalamus sends a signal to the pituitary gland saying "Urgent! Get the adrenals up and release stress hormones, adrenaline and cortisol, IMMEDIATE ACTION REQUIRED"
2. Your heart starts pounding, your pupils dilate, your airways open up and your logical brain is put temporarily offline.

3. You're ready to fight anything or run faster than a rocket. You're ready – on high alert.

Picture the scenario where the bear in the woods is you're unpredictable alcoholic mother. Adrenaline has kicked into action daily, and you become unable to differentiate real and perceived dangers. The result is that your brain becomes ready to react to the smell of lager (or whatever) and a pathway is opened up in the neural structures.

Any treatment needs to enable that pathway to become a cul-de-sac and a new pathway created, where the adrenals are pushed, only when there genuinely IS a "bear in the woods" scenario unfolding.

That is neuroplasticity – and the good news is that whilst in the past it was regarded as futile to attempt to change neural pathways in an adult, now, it is seen that new pathways can be (and are) created fast, and old ones closed down.

There is no doubt that some of the neural motorways of the past (such as fear of men for example, so that you refrain from ever trusting one) do become cul-de-sacs. You will no doubt turn onto that road periodically, but rapidly realise the futile nature of that neural pathway, re-join the new main road and realise that the trust issue was to do with a particular man (in this example – it could equally be a woman)

It really is as simple as that. So how can it be fixed? Reprogramming the brain and neural pathways sounds expensive, painful and extreme, but in truth, it's quite simple. To get the brain to notice the Bear has a shabby fur coat and its big teeth are painful to the bear for instance.

[9]

So, what can help enable fast neuroplasticity? None of the methods mentioned in this book are in conflict, they all fit well with each other. Mindfulness and Limbic Reflexology are mentioned but there are better places than here to research these techniques. I mention them for completeness. Constellations is my own field of work and study and so the part of this book that covers constellations is a great deal more comprehensive. Find tools that work for you, and use them.

Flower Essences

Flower essences are used to establish balance in the emotional body. Naturally this has an impact on the mental, physical and spiritual bodies. Allowing the systems to relax and engage with change is something that flower essences are very good at. Look at www.lotusholistic.com (my wife Julie Bowman's website – she is an advanced practitioner, and a producer too)

Mindfulness

Mindfulness means paying attention on purpose to the present moment with compassion curiosity and acceptance. So, you may be feeling tired and anxious. The acceptance of that is quite liberating, and the compassion you then go on to give yourself reduces both the anxiety and the tiredness. Regular mindfulness meditation, often as simple as giving yourself genuine time to reflect on the here and now, will engage with neuroplasticity and enable permanent neural pathway changes. A crucial part of mindfulness is honesty with oneself. To persistently avoid looking at your own system, shame, guilt, strengths and weaknesses will only make matters worse.

Limbic Reflexology
From www.limbicreflexology.co.uk

"Limbic Reflexology focuses on the reflex areas on the feet pertaining to the subcortical structures and nuclei of the brain, which are largely responsible for filtering information from our external, and internal world, and for generating our autonomic and behaviour responses to that information. This includes our emotional responses and our response to our experience of pain. These structures and nuclei are commonly referred to as the limbic brain.

In 2011, I accidently discovered a reflex area, that was unfamiliar to me. I looked at various maps, but none gave me a clue as to its identity. However, when worked, there was a dramatic and significant, beneficial change for the client. For some time, it baffled me, but after reading an article in New Scientist, it dawned on me, that it may well be the reflex area for the Amygdala, a subcortical nucleus of the brain. The effect of working It, was to reduce the hyper-arousal effects of anxiety. I began to find it on other clients, with a similar beneficial effect. The Amygdala seemed to be the prime candidate.

Based on this hypothesis, and taking the pituitary as a reference point, I looked for other reflex areas in the places where I ought to find them. I did discover others, but establishing their identity, and mapping those reflex areas, presented a confusing picture. The Amygdala was in the wrong place.

The answer came after exploring the developing brain of the human embryo. By tilting the angle of the brain, the identity of the

[11]

reflex areas become clearer, and they all fell into place. My 'Amygdala' turned out to be the Insula, with the amygdala reflex area close by.

The significance of Limbic Reflexology became clearer, with the discovery of a pattern of tender reflex areas, in a variety of conditions. By cross referencing, it became possible to identify each reflex area.

Since those initial findings, we now have over thirty discrete reflex areas, and I have no doubt, that in time, more will reveal themselves.

The Amygdala, Insular Cortex, Hippocampus, Hypothalamus, Thalamus, Cingulate Cortex, Locus Coeruleus, Periaqueductal Grey, Raphe Nucleus, BNST, Nucleus Accumbens and Striatum are some of the current candidates for the discrete reflex areas that make up the jigsaw."

Hamish Edgar – website and book

Google each of these, and the significance of Limbic Reflexology will become clear.

Constellations

So how can a constellation help? You will need to read the chapters on constellation work to fully understand the process, unless of course you have experienced such methods. For a child, the unpredictable alcoholic mother assumes massive proportions, and is to be feared. As an adult in the context of a constellation, the relationship switches and the scale vastly diminish, and the power balance is restored so that we can work on some ceremonies and rituals to further resource you and reduce the issue. The key that will arise of itself is to remain loyal to some parts of the story, and hugely disloyal to others. The unpredictable alcoholic mother did give you life, and if you are reading this book, or seeking help you no doubt want to run your life better without the guilt, shame and memories. In a constellation, the process could lead to a bit of work where the representative of you, says to the representative of your mother "Thank you for my life, I got enough, the rest I leave with you" It might be followed by you taking your place in the "constellation" and repeating the sentence. Sounds simple, but I have seen close to a hundred people take that place, say those words (or similar) and feel changed in that moment. Why? Well, you need to read the chapter on epigenetics. And remarkably, I have seen a number of those people some years later who report that the change stuck. Or to put it scientifically, the neural pathway got dug up! And a permanent diversion notice was placed.

Positive Effects from ACEs

One major impact from high ACEs that is positive, provided that the individual can achieve the shift, is that constantly being on guard means that you may develop high levels of intuition. The

[13]

origin of sight appears to be many millions of years of touch gradually changing into senses that didn't need quite such a physical connection. The same is true of intuition – sensing something that others may be oblivious to. The individual begins to sense as he or she comes home from the bus stop, that today is a bad day. In that moment the strategies that are most likely to work, kick in, and the individual builds the best protection available PRIOR to the event that would certainly have triggered.

The key to escaping the prison sentence of high ACE scores seems to be resilience. Just as the surviving tadpoles develop legs early, so the resilient adult uses the knowledge and understanding to grow empathy where resentment existed prior. (see page 20 for the article on tadpoles in a drying out pond in relation to resilience)

Also see later under resentment.

Loyalty

Loyalty is a complex matter and causes considerable problems of psychological wellbeing in later life. Essentially, humans are expected to evolve gradually (like all complex animals) so loyalty is built into the system. Simpler animals can get all they need from genetics, so for example, a salmon if brought up from egg to adult in a completely isolated environment away from any previous environments, and indeed from any other salmon, it will behave very much like any other salmon, and may even finds its way back to the stream it was actually hatched in - perhaps many hundreds of miles distant. So why are humans different? The complexity of the human (and other high order mammals) means that there are many things that need to be learned and accommodated.

The brain of the human has developed over history and prehistory. It also develops considerably during a person's lifetime. Thus, the baby has a far simpler brain than the one that it has as an adult. The skull will need to enlarge to accommodate the new space requirements. The limbic part of the brain is primordial and has simple structures that engage the adrenals and the cortisol (stress hormones) in the body. The baby won't need reasoning skills till much later, so initially it is completely dependent on the mother function (that is not necessarily provided by the genetic mother, nor even a female). He or she will need food, warmth and love for survival. For the adult to set aside a good deal of freedom to assist in that process, the bonding is started by some hormonal changes in the mother. This is clearly much more likely to occur if the mothering is undertaken by the biological mother, but it has been shown to occur in foster mothers of babies too. The satisfaction of need by the baby creates hormonal changes of bonding too. And so, it begins. The expectations are that safety, warmth and nurturing will all arrive for the baby in ample abundance. Emotional, mental, physical and spiritual wellbeing come out of that appropriate start in life, and the bonding is complete, and the mother becomes the best role model of a woman for the child, and the father becomes the best role model of a man for the child. So, when the male child grows up, he is likely to partner up with someone resembling his mother, and the girl child equally is likely to partner up with someone resembling her father. And this will have developed with epigenetics (Epigenetics is the study of heritable changes in gene expression (active versus inactive genes) that do not involve changes to the underlying DNA sequence — a change in phenotype without a change in genotype — which in turn affects how cells read the genes. (source: http://whatisepigenetics.com)

So far so good. The species develops gradually due to hard wired coding that states that relationships should be based on the best role models – your parents. So, children grow believing that the experience they had or have is normal, so what they will expect in a relationship is what they already know relationships to look and feel like. So, the little girl with an abusive father is highly likely to seek abusive men in her adulthood – out of loyalty.

The other trick that is played out in the human psyche is that guilt and shame are used (see next section) as a tool to keep the loyalties tight, rather than allowing the child in this case to see the bigger picture, or a perspective on loyalty to a wider system (society at large for instance). "You can't tell anyone, or things will be worse" etc.

In a later chapter on constellations (my particular method of choice for repairing damage done by high score ACE's) I talk about being highly selective about loyalty. It is entirely in order to say to a representative version of your highly abusive father "Thank you for my life, I got enough. The rest I leave with you". What's the point? Well it allows the individual to establish that life itself is good, but some of the experiences of an abusive father (in this example) had nothing to do with me. The work that leads up to genuine statements of this sort can be long winded, or quite short, but either way it is profound. The realisation of decades of malfunctioning neural pathways can be extraordinarily liberating. This requires the neo cortex to be fully developed, and this development occurs later in life. The statement hands back the issue of the abuse to the father (in this example) leaving the child of that abusive father to relish and enjoy the life that was given without the pain of the abuse. It seems to be remarkably effective.

Guilt and Shame

What's the difference between Guilt and Shame? To paraphrase Brene Brown

Shame says "I am a bad person for doing such and such"

Guilt says "I did a bad thing"

(excellent ted talk - https://www.ted.com/talks/brene_brown_listening_to_shame?language=en)

We all experience Guilt and Shame, but why? Why is it so common? Well, the simple answer is that it's a tool used by systems and controlling members of the system to control behaviour that might render the system at risk.

Let me explain. We live in a society with rules, such us "Thou shalt not steal". In an older civilisation, or perhaps pre-civilisation when ownership of stuff hadn't been invented, stealing hadn't been invented either. The indigenous peoples of pre 19th century America had no concept of ownership of land, hence when settlers arrived who did have that concept there was trouble. Initially the Native Americans didn't understand the very idea of owning land. The guilt imposed by society protects the system by helping people feel guilty if they were about to steal something. Shame has the after effect – "You've brought shame on our family...."

So that's a good use – it helps valid societies keep stable and protects it from subversion. But what about its misuse? When parents humiliate, hurt or otherwise deliberately pass shame to absolve them of guilt, or to keep the story of life at home under wraps, they create a network of issues. John Bradshaw in his book "Healing the shame that binds us" he talks of the way systems can be protected by misuse of this tool. It is often used as a tool to keep family secrets secret. It is used as a tool to keep a little girl from telling her mum that she is being abused by her dad. "if you tell anyone our little secret, you'll be taken into care, the family will be broken up ant it'll be all your fault" - guilt and shame at its worst.

When the amygdala is fired too frequently, the extra stimulation of cortisol (stress hormone) in early childhood can affect all parts of the system. The range of potential symptoms go from bed wetting, stunting growth in early life to reducing life expectancy by as much as 20 years. See Nadine Burke Harris TEDMED talk (YouTube https://www.youtube.com/watch?v=95ovIJ3dsNk)

The simple number of Adverse Childhood Experiences seems to affect the extent to which cortisol is produced in later life, and too much will hurt you. The evidence seems to point to the idea that if your brain is bombarded with different adverse experiences it responds in deeper and deeper ways, so that the effects become more complicated and difficult to a) address and b) counteract.

Talking therapies, limbic reflexology, mindful meditation, family constellation work will all change the way that the body attends to stress and can modify the archive storage of stress memory stimulated by the hippocampus when stress scenarios are triggered. The key is that you will need to engage with neuroplasticity one way or another if you are going to reduce the impact and stop the flooding of the system with toxic levels of cortisol and adrenalin.

Resentment

"Resentment is like drinking poison and then hoping it will kill your enemies." — Nelson Mandela

The statement by Nelson Mandela sums up the whole issue of resentment. The issue is that people have expectations – the 2-year-old expects a hug, the schoolboy expects to be rewarded for good work, and the graduate expects to be admired and celebrated. In my own case my mother didn't attend my degree ceremony after achieving a BA Hons after 4 years study, stating that "Bristol Polytechnic was not a proper university!" (she went to St Andrews) and my father ostensibly didn't come for the same reasons but actually he failed matriculation and never attended any higher education, and from persistently stating that I would never amount to anything in different ways, was probably shamed himself had he come to my graduation. His expectations were so high that after failing all my 'O' Levels twice and being sent to a "crammer" to get some O levels under pressure, I sat English Language 'O' level with two different exam boards, because I didn't have the results of my first when I was due to sit the next (the expectation passed to me was that I would yet again, fail!. By the way I passed both!

Fortunately, I was a bright kid, and not easily floored, and decided that enough was enough, so I played truant and got odd jobs at the nearby Earls Court Exhibition centre. When eventually I returned to the crammer to get my grades, I was told that I had missed many lessons and therefore they owed me a refund – how did I want it paid! (I called that a result!) – see the tadpoles example below - I had grown legs!

Epigenetics affect the way we respond. I could have built that persistent knock back policy of my father into a depressing rotation of resentment and self-harm (not necessarily physical self-harm) and used sabotage as the power tool of psychology to be in charge of the things that would likely fail. We all use sabotage sometimes, but it failed to become a deeply rooted problem for me.

A study of tadpoles in a pond that is drying out shows that there is a watershed moment in the development. If the pond dries out a little too soon, the tadpoles do not flourish and die out – becoming food for predators rapidly. If the development of the tadpoles has passed a notional critical point, the tadpoles grow legs much faster and escape the dried-out pond. In my case I grew legs early! It never became resentment – indeed I would go so far as to say my father's attitudes were turned into a gift – but I was just into my sixties before I consciously saw it in that way. His view was that I should always strive to improve (a noble ambition) but in excess it became debilitating such that I would always fail to achieve. Later I realised that it meant I had no end goals, and just engaged with process. Thus, for the work I do now, I have no identified position at the start, and any outcome is satisfactory. Thus, I am liberated form feelings of disappointment if I don't get to a known expected place – which would be horribly limiting in the field I work in. My careers have often been practical but always in the frame of "am I enjoying the journey?" rather than "am I achieving my goals?"

Sabotage

Sabotage is a tool used by people to gain power. If they are likely to fail, or be hurt, they can take control by doing it themselves - the control has been taken away from others and put back with the individual. Many aspects of a high ACEs score will involve powerlessness, and sabotage becomes the tool of choice in many of those situations.

Sometimes (especially psychosexual trauma) the individual must shut down their feelings completely to endure the humiliation, guilt and shame of their experience. Self-harm is often conducted to engage with being able to feel and going back to a primitive idea of feeling in the physical sense rather than the later developed emotional, mental and spiritual sense.

ACEs Scoring

Research done in the 1980s and 90s revealed a direct causal link between early childhood trauma otherwise known as adverse childhood experience (ACEs) and chronic health issues later in life and even life expectancy research carried out in South San Francisco had a cohort of 17,000 people.

The consolidation research by Nadine Burke Harris in her TED talks and in her book the Deepest Well demonstrates knowledge that wasn't picked up on in prior years. Her research and work brings together the original 17,000 cohort study in Sothern California, a study of 1,000 people in New Zealand monitored over thirty years, tadpoles developing new limbs early, or not surviving depending on when their pond dries out, and rats licking their babies – it turns out high licking rats offspring will be high lickers, and low licking rats will have low licking babies. (That's unless babies get switched, in which case babies follow step mum). If you stress a baby rat, and pass it back to its mother, the baby will produce cortisol in direct negative correlation with the degree that the mother licks it. The more licks the baby rat gets. the less cortisol it needs to produce and the less licks the baby rat gets, the more cortisol it will need to sort out the stress it has been subjected to. Rats born to low lickers will become low lickers (apparently genetics) but actually, fostered rats behave and reproduce like their foster parent – hence it must be epigenetics – i.e. developed during lifetime as a component of the genetic code that gets passed on to the next generation. Sounds extraordinary but in truth this is a start of the new wave of healing that is a recognition of the connection between your start in life and the end of life and in my opinion is overdue.

This is using epigenetic modification as a tool to correct adverse epigenetic changes. "How?" is the theme of this little book.

What's Your ACE Score?

There are 10 types of childhood trauma measured in the ACE Study. Five are personal — physical abuse, verbal abuse, sexual abuse, physical neglect, and emotional neglect. Five are related to other family members: a parent who's an alcoholic, a mother who's a victim of domestic violence, a family member in jail, a family member diagnosed with a mental illness, and the disappearance of a parent through divorce, death or abandonment. Each type of trauma counts as one. So, a person who's been physically abused, with one alcoholic parent, and a mother who was beaten up has an ACE score of three. Witnessing trauma is sometimes just as damaging, and in my own experience with clients, sometimes harder to deal with – the client gets locked into an idea that "at least it wasn't happening to me". However, their own feeling of powerlessness dramatically increases the issues that they will have faced.

There are, of course, many other types of childhood trauma — racism, bullying, watching a sibling being abused, losing a caregiver (grandmother, mother, grandfather, etc.),

[23]

homelessness, surviving and recovering from a severe accident, witnessing a father being abused by a mother, witnessing a grandmother abusing a father, involvement with the foster care system, involvement with the juvenile justice system, etc. The ACE Study included only those 10 childhood traumas because those were mentioned as most common by a group of about 300 Kaiser members; those traumas were also well studied individually in the research literature. Also, the extent of the research using that set of issues means it remains comparable.

The most important thing to remember is that the ACE score is meant as a guideline: If you experienced other types of toxic stress over months or years, then those would likely increase your risk of health consequences.

Worth remembering is that the different types of stresses rather than the quantity of similar stress incidents is the key to understanding the way the brain builds up the production of cortisol. In the cases of early sexual abuse in cases I personally have observed, the cases where there was repeated similar instances over a protracted period seem to enable the client's brain to engage. There is little confusion about what happened and the only question that might be difficult to answer would be how many times? When did it start? When did it stop? The client with a very small number of incidences, or the client who maybe witnessed something once, and was then repeated told it never happened, may find it very difficult to engage and hence may get stress hormones poured into the system to a) cover the experience, and b) cover the confusion. These cases are sometimes more difficult to manage.

Epigenetics

This book is NOT designed to explain complex scientific models, or to expand on knowledge well established in the outside world. However, for the purposes of this book, epigenetics needs a little explanation.

The implication of common belief is that we have DNA which holds the key to all that we inherit and have to live with. In other words, our fate. People talk of strong DNA etc.

The truth is a bit more complicated. The DNA is encoded into genes clustered together into chromosomes and certain factors prescribe how we develop. EG in most mammals and some insects' males have an X and a Y chromosome (they are different shapes and sizes) and females have two of the same type of X chromosome. There are some other determinants for sexual identity, but this book is not the place for that.

If you liken the chromosomes to cars travelling around, then it can be seen that a safe healthy childhood with little adversity will enable the bumpers on the car to remain intact, colourful and robust for when the occasional bump does occur. The bumpers on the car where multiple serious pileups have occurred will mean far less ability in later life to withstand the bumps of normal life. The bumpers in epigenetics are called histone and they play a role in DNA regulation, and hence add to the picture of life going forward, hence the multi-generational aspect of adversity. It has been shown that many issues developed in one generation will pass to the next unless they are dealt with. As the code gets enhanced and added to along the way, sometimes the issues get worse through that process. There are many cases of a serial killer being a person who had a terrible and abusive childhood, but as you can see, the issues in the earlier generation were singular, the issues of the subsequent generation, multiple and consequently, worse.

Systems thinking

What is a system, and what do we mean by it in this context? A system is any identifiable group of people or even things. WE all belong to family of origin with an essential mother and father – without whom we would not exist at all. How they managed the pressures of that world is possibly the subject of a constellation for the reader! If the reader has a high ACEs score, then clearly the parents mismanaged their own system somewhat. (see my book "Family Constellations - Unravelling the mystery of your ancestral timeline" http://books.rafenauen.com). But that is just one system that we belong to and constellation work holds good in ANY system, be it a school, a prison, a workplace or your family group. All systems are defined by the rules of belonging and the loyalties that pertain. All systems on close inspection have distinct rules – in my family, for instance we were expected to talk "properly". Failure to observe that rule alone had consequences, and so it is with all systems, be it a subscription must be paid to a club for instance, and people may speculate what rules applied to be a member of the Waffen SS. Rules can change over time. Until recently a rule in England stated that marriages consist only of one man and one woman. The rules now allow for two people of the same sex. A system therefore is any group defined by the relationship they have to each other – family, workgroup, board of directors and so on. In much of my work, I am dealing with family systems, but the rules apply to any grouping of people or things that might be regarded as a system – even down to a chronic illness. By way of example someone has a painful broken leg. Clearly the problem is in the leg, or perhaps they are even more precise and say their knee is the issue, but their lack of mobility will have a profound effect on what they are able to do. They might have suffered some severe trauma getting the original damage to the knee, so could have nightmares, quite apart from the normal sleep deprivation from pain. That may mean that they get annoyed or upset more than would be normal for them. The family then will have to rally round – transport, maybe the bedroom is inaccessible so things will change in the house, and maybe there is a sudden drop in income that coincides with a sudden increase in costs, so worry in the family will increase. So, you can see that looking at basic elements on their own is a far from perfect way to arrive at successful outcomes, and sometimes it can be far more useful to look at the system. Thus, it can be demonstrated that the broken leg is a systemic issue, and the confines of the observation will simply relate to how wide you look.

Systemic Constellations – what are they?

The fundamentals

So, what is a constellation (apart from a group of stars)? – well fundamentally, it's a living map that reveals the hidden dynamics of any system.

A Constellation is an experiential model for looking into the mechanics of any system. By experiential I mean to say that all the outcomes appear from the work itself – there is no formulae for the outcomes from the observable inputs – so the facilitator needs to have the confidence to simply observe and let the work take its course, with gentle guidance rather than determined manipulations.

The starting point is always someone who wants to look at an issue, perhaps there's a recurrent problem at work, or some situation that they can't quite come to grips with. It may be a forced change within the system – a death, a birth, a marriage or a divorce, or "problems" with a child's behaviour may becoming noticeably difficult to deal with.

They may have experienced a noticeable pattern of unsuitable or even abusive partners. Noticing patterns that need to change is often the key that will start to unlock the doors to the system.

Constellations are a powerful way of working with such issues, and as they work entirely on systems, and yet require no distinct knowledge of what or how the symptoms of the issues arose from that system, they are an extremely valuable tool. In this book, of course, it will a high Aces score that prompts "taking a look". Rather than look at the individual or the place where the problem is, we look at the whole system. That's because an individual is always part of a much wider interconnected system, and the problem may just be a symptom of something that's happening elsewhere.

The Mechanics of a workshop

What we do is set up a visual spatial representation of that system. Ideally, we use people to represent the different parts of the system so it becomes a living map or constellation, but pieces of felt on a floor; post it notes; specially manufactured directional pieces of plastic or wood; or even PlayPeople™ can be used. We then ask those representatives to listen to their feelings, their sensations and their intuitions and what happens is that the underlying dynamics of the system come to the surface. It seems that simply giving the client permission for an element of their existence to be represented is enough for the display of the dynamics to begin. Many hundreds of thousands of workshops have been noted and written up, and they all show that some hidden dynamics have been revealed that have lain hidden previously. In the case of plastic pieces, the client places the representative blocks as he sees fit, and the facilitator has to do a bit more work to engage with the system, and to begin any dialogue.

[29]

Who is in a constellation?

The facilitator – someone who guides the process, but who remains as far as possible, outside the process

A seeker - someone who feels the urge to look at their stuff, right now – they will probably be a bit fired up, enthusiastic – their moment has arrived.

Representatives – people who will get asked to represent other people during the process – placeholders certainly, but sometimes quite a bit more

Participants – the rest of the people in the workshop – they sit around the edge of the working area and hold the energy – they just observe mostly – they will get a chance to be a seeker, or a participant later

Only the facilitator will necessarily have had prior experience of constellation work, but some, maybe all of the others will have attended workshops before – even participants get a big learning from the work.

What happens in a constellation workshop?

In the "people" example of a constellation, everyone sits around in a circle of chairs – preferably about eighteen to twenty feet across the circle. The facilitator will have picked a place to sit and have a vacant chair next to him or her. He or she will probably do a short meditation, so that everyone is calm, relaxed and body conscious – by that I mean that people become aware of what is going on in their own body, so that they can express changes that occur – these may become quite important as the work progresses. The circle inside the chairs is called the field – like a field of energy and is identified to establish boundaries to the work.

Firstly, a seeker is chosen. The facilitator may choose, or ask "who is ready?", or maybe another method is used. The seeker comes and sits by the facilitator. The conversation that ensues is simply to establish who are the important players in the system described by the client – it will obviously involve a mother father and the client's representative if the work is dealing with family of origin.

It is not crucial for the process to continue to have that conversation at all. Constellations work on the hidden dynamics, not the known expressions of existent dynamics.

Why runs a constellation?

Having established that a) there are laws, and b) that they may have been offended in some in the past and that c) balance being restored without someone having to say commit suicide in the system, it seems obvious to do something. Normal counselling and coaching focusses on the client and aspects that are directly in contact or have been in contact with the client – past histories and landscapes may express an influence that is noted, but in the constellation model, all aspects of the life and work of the client,

[31]

all the histories and contexts can be externally represented so that an overview becomes much clearer – even in respect of things that are unknown.

Every child that has been adopted, will obviously have had a birth mother and father for a time – they may have died, they may be living another life elsewhere, and the counsellor or therapist may be stuck with the shame blame betrayal or abandonment issues that the client presents. The constellation model is able to notice that the client is alive, well, and in that sense, successful, and therefore got everything they needed to be exactly who they are – in constellation modelling words "they got enough" – and that revelation can be of enormous value and be sincerely empowering. All the shame blame betrayal or abandonment can be shed, and the client feels entirely different, permanently from that moment.

Tools for the job

Constellations can use a variety of tools to externally represent the inner workings of a system.

1. People – in a workshop the distinct advantage of using people to represent other people from within a system, is that they can talk and express verbally, and emotionally aspects that they gather from the permission given to them. The facilitator is able to ask direct questions and get direct answers that come from the felt sense of the placing within the constellation and does not require asking the client about things that show up but that may remain unexplained.

[32]

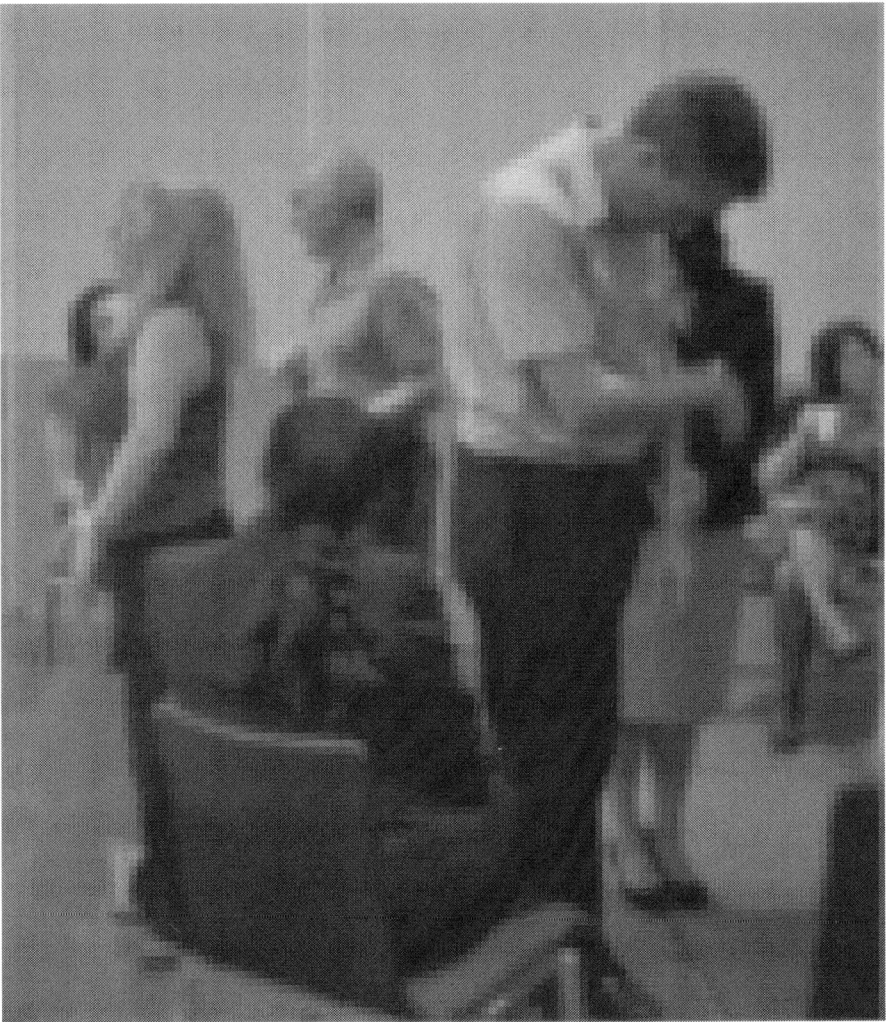

Facilitator needs to notice things that interest or disinterest participants and any sorrow that shows up. This is easier with people participants than with other methods.

2. Horses – there are some constellation facilitators that use horses to represent, and although this admittedly seems extreme, some excellent results have been observed. The horse cannot verbalise but can express resistances, sorrow

[33]

and indeed enthusiasm. The advantage is that horses whilst being external sentient beings in the work, they are removed from the perceived problem of participants who appear to have their own agenda. (In fact, that is almost never an issue as they tend to represent agendas in their correct context!)

3. Felt squares – these can be very useful here a client is extremely nervous of expressing deep inner conflicts – for example the child that results from a rape may have such a sense of shame and anger that the very idea of a group context might prevent the work ever being done. If the client is a girl she may identify with the mother and have very difficult relationships with men, and the work may be done when she is an adult. In that particular scenario the best outcome is for the child to notice that but for the rape, she would not even exist and that being alive is far

better than to never have been born. Thus, she gets to the ideal place where she thanks her mother for the ordeal that she had to endure for her to be born, and to thank her father for the gift of life, even if it required those particular circumstances.

The shame, blame and anger dissipate without further ado.

The client has stepped on each square to identify with each person or aspect being enquired into. The resulting shapes then yield information to take new steps in towards resolution.

4. Wooden blocks – very useful in business scenarios where changes to personnel can be tried out without cost to the business and without interference. In these cases, the client does all the work with a little guidance and hopefully very little influence. Managers who find themselves out on a limb may discover what is really going on in their workgroup without having to ask the team any awkward

[35]

questions that might of themselves endanger the working relationship.

5. Post it notes – very useful for light touch constellation work so that the client can move stuff around very simply on a table
6. Chocolate bars! – I did a very useful constellation in a coffee shop, and the tools to hand where cheap choc bars – which we used to show where the reason for lack customers came from – the whole focus of the management was on satisfying the bank – they had forgotten staff and customers and quality of product was looking to leave the system – and remember it was the manager moving the bars around – it's just externalising that inner knowing that everyone already knows uses and experiences daily
7. PlayPeople™ - very useful for children. The facilitator can safely introduce them back into a traumatic scenario to enable them to feel empowered by putting them in

[36]

control of outcomes. The youngest child I have worked with in this context was three and his mum and dad had split up and daddy had a new girlfriend. The mum was concerned that he would be confused, hurt and angry. What showed up, was lovely and simple and four years on, the mother still feels happy and the mother and the father communicate easily on matters pertaining to the little boy. That's not always the case. In another constellation a little girl who had been frightened in her parents break up by police, fire engines and medical staff and when we did the work she put all the "blue lights" (her words not mine) into a toy bucket, so that she could bring them in as she saw fit – it enabled her to slow down all the actions and reactions so that she stayed in control. The outcome was a far less frightened five-year-old child.

Extraordinarily – even PlayPeople™ figures appear to display feelings when placed in constellations – here one figure is representing someone who died, and at least one figure appears to not wish to look!

[37]

8. Anything! – you can use anything. Preferably the items used will have some directional quality – review of the patterns is much easier if you can easily see which way everyone is facing.

Scope of constellation work

It is clear from massive amounts of research in numerous categories that provided that what is being asked is of a systemic nature, constellation model will add to the value and simplicity of the answer.

Family

Many of the examples herein are attributed to family systems. For further reading see the bibliography for my first book in this series – Family Constellations – Unravelling the Mystery of your ancestral Timeline – available in paperback and on Kindle.

Stephan Hausner in his practice of Chinese medicine, Homeopathy and Osteopathy that many clients displayed hidden patterns that appeared to come from families where there seemed little possibility of genetic transference across generations. Extensive correspondence with Bert Hellinger enlightened that aspect and Stephan went on to study and practice his constellation work in the field of chronic health. His book "Even if it costs me my life" is a book with many case studies and references. Often, in the best of interests, things that happened are hidden. Such things might be an abortion that was foisted on a teenager. The inability to grieve or to represent that love that she felt will never disappear but instead, an illness or physical anomaly may occur. The constellation of those aspects enables the grieving to take place, and more importantly, the client to take his or her place in the life and system to which they belong, and the need to pass the entanglement to yet another generation seems to completely disappear.

Sometimes a person will take on the illness of another, almost by demand. In this example I am using a woman in her mid-fifties. Her children have left home, her libido has changed and her mother in her eighties is having some eyesight issues. The client feels less needed and respected in this phase – she has yet to have grandchildren and her mother begins to need transporting around. The client feels a normal debt of gratitude to her mother who raised her "in difficult circumstances". She begins to say out loud "Don't worry mum, I'll do it for you". She begins to say to her friends that she could cope with the illness her mother begins to experience, better than her mother. She begins to say, "I'll carry the illness for you". It is unlikely that her statements are quite as direct, but the intention is set. The outcome is that the client gets ill too, and then feels terrible that she cannot look after her mother either, and she hasn't helped her mother's illness. This feeling responsible for the care of others is for the client to feel towards children and grandchildren, not for parents, but the issue of parenting parents has become endemic in many western societies. The constellation enables the client to see the futility of such behaviour in the context of the health and wellbeing of the system and can therefore inhabit a richer world.

The fundamental laws of being Human

There appear to be natural laws for humans that have been closely observed over many years, and from many situations, not

[39]

to mention the thousands of constellation workshops that have been recorded where these aspects pertain. Many of these aspects could well come under the heading common sense, but quite a few have unexpected elements.

We all accept that the law of gravity exists, and we don't have to continually check to see if it is in operation. The human laws appear to be a little subtler, and hence many people will fail to notice, sometimes repeatedly. For instance, there is a law that what comes later takes precedence over what comes before. This law is there to ensure that youngest children get what they need – a one year old is less at risk than a 3-day old. However, it also means that a man who has a child within an affair possibly believes he has choices over who to stay with – and in truth he probably doesn't – eventually he will discover that the child that came last takes precedence. The world is littered with the results of ignoring that law!

So, what are these laws?

1. Everyone has an equal right to belong - everyone who enters a system (a new baby for example) has a right to as much love as anyone else, and it can be shown that having "favourites" causes issues down the line. It seems from extensive scrutiny that the system always manages to balance out any imbalances that have been injected into the system – for instance when a child is forgotten, somewhere a repeat of the situation or similar may recur.

2. Things that come before have to give way to things that come later - an older sibling has to allow his or her world to change a little for the survival of the system, and his or

[40]

her place within it. That ensures that growing systems do not have built in neglect.

3. Later systems take precedence over older systems. If someone has a child in the context of an affair, it can be pretty harsh for the original family system. The person who has partially moved away and into a new system, will have much more energy for the new system, whatever they say to themselves, or whatever promises they may make. This especially shows up as an issue when the apparently aggrieved party appears to know nothing of the affair – people looking on who know the whole truth will notice how the system tried to reveal in undercurrents so that the truth avails itself.

4. The balance of giving and receiving needs to be maintained - common sense (and a great deal of research) has shown that balance must be maintained in all things, especially family systems. Research of a phenomenon in America looking into why training doctors often appeared to leave wives just as they qualified. What became clear was that the partner gave up a great deal for the training partner to succeed, who went on to believe they could never repay the cost of that gift to them. The balance could only be satisfied by them leaving, otherwise they would always be in debt to the giver, which would imbalance the system. Harsh, but no less true for that.

These laws can easily be broken – here are a few examples:

- when babies are aborted or stillborn and not mourned or talked about

- when children or young adults die and are not mourned
- when children are given away for adoption and no longer talked about
- when adoptive parents do not acknowledge the natural parents of their children
- when previous partners or important relationships are not acknowledged and honoured between couples
- when extra-marital relationships are kept secret
- when the experiences of war are not remembered and the dead honoured
- when there are family secrets
- when ACEs scores are high

Constellations rely on some underlying principles - a bit like a house relies on gravity.

1.   Everyone has an equal right to belong - everyone who enters a system (a new baby for example) has a right to as much love as anyone else, and it can be shown that having "favourites" causes issues down the line

2.   Things that come before have to give way to things that come later - an older sibling must allow his or her world to change a little for the survival of the system, and his or her place within it.

[42]

3. Later systems take precedence over older systems. If someone has a child in the context of an affair, it can be harsh for the original family system. The person who has partially moved away and into a new system, will have much more energy for the new system, whatever they say to themselves, or whatever promises they may make.

4. The balance of giving and receiving needs to be maintained - common sense (and a great deal of research) has shown that balance must be maintained in all things, especially family systems.

What are the limitations?

Technically none, but there are provisos. A system is likely to overlap other systems, and it behoves the facilitator to respect the boundaries of any system. I belong to my family of origin, my first children's marriage, my second children's marriage, my third marriage, my spiritual support group, I am a UK citizen and I have a credit card and a four bank accounts. So that's 11 with no thought, and most people are the same. Obviously, RBS are not involved with my family of origin and it would be out of place to include it in work about my family, but other arenas may be less obvious. We do have permission to represent my second wife at any stage because she died, but my first wife is alive, and therefore could only come up legitimately in a constellation to do with my eldest (and her) children.

Neuroplasticity

Neuroplasticity: The brain's ability to reorganize itself by forming new neural connections throughout life. Neuroplasticity allows the neurons (nerve cells) in the brain to compensate for injury and disease and to adjust their activities in response to new situations or to changes in their environment.

Brain reorganization takes place by mechanisms such as "axonal sprouting" in which undamaged axons grow new nerve endings to reconnect neurons whose links were injured or severed. Undamaged axons can also sprout nerve endings and connect with other undamaged nerve cells, forming new neural pathways to accomplish a needed function.

For example, if one hemisphere of the brain is damaged, the intact hemisphere may take over some of its functions. The brain compensates for damage in effect by reorganizing and forming new connections between intact neurons. In order to reconnect, the neurons need to be stimulated through activity.

Neuroplasticity sometimes may also contribute to impairment. For example, people who are deaf may suffer from a continual ringing in their ears (tinnitus), the result of the rewiring of brain cells starved for sound. For neurons to form beneficial connections, they must be correctly stimulated.

Neuroplasticity is also called brain plasticity or brain malleability. (Source Medicinenet.com)

Encouraging overall calm using mindfulness and meditation has been shown to enable the neurons to build new pathways. Undoubtedly toxic stress is the one thing most likely to interrupt such repair.

Also, Constellations seem to adjust the mindset rapidly such that the seeker can separate the loyalties that are supportive from the loyalties that are toxic. A seeker is a client or person who is interested in adjusting their systems view to better support their life's purpose. In that way, the seeker can waymark their neural pathways for closure, and give some warning of the consequences of "going down that road again". It seems to work remarkably fast, and the understanding of why and how is limited – it is only the sheer volume of results that can be used to make a case for this methodology to be used.

Appendices

ACEs Scoring Sheet

Prior to your 18th birthday:

1. Did a parent or other adult in the household often or very often... Swear at you, insult you, put you down, or humiliate you? or Act in a way that made you afraid that you might be physically hurt?
   No___If Yes, enter 1 ___
2. Did a parent or other adult in the household often or very often... Push, grab, slap, or throw something at you? or Ever hit you so hard that you had marks or were injured?
   No___If Yes, enter 1 ___
3. Did an adult or person at least 5 years older than you ever... Touch or fondle you or have you touch their body in a sexual way? or Attempt or actually have oral, anal, or vaginal intercourse with you?
   No___If Yes, enter 1 ___
4. Did you often or very often feel that ... No one in your family loved you or thought you were important or special? or Your family didn't look out for each other, feel close to each other, or support each other?
   No___If Yes, enter 1 ___
5. Did you often or very often feel that ... You didn't have enough to eat, had to wear dirty clothes, and had no one to protect you? or Your parents were too drunk or high to take care of you or take you to the doctor if you needed it?
   No___If Yes, enter 1 __
6. Were your parents ever separated or divorced?
   No___If Yes, enter 1 ___
7. Was your mother or stepmother:
   Often or very often pushed, grabbed, slapped, or had something thrown at her? or Sometimes, often, or very often kicked, bitten, hit with a fist, or hit with something hard? or Ever repeatedly hit over at least a few minutes or

threatened with a gun or knife?

No___If Yes, enter 1 ___

8. Did you live with anyone who was a problem drinker or alcoholic, or who used street drugs?

   No___If Yes, enter 1 ___

9. Was a household member depressed or mentally ill, or did a household member attempt

   suicide?   No___If Yes, enter 1 ___

10. Did a household member go to prison?

    No___If Yes, enter 1 ___

Bibliography

Hamish Edgar - Limbic Reflexology: Student Textbook Revised Edition
Nadine Burke Harris – Deepest Well
Julia Buckley – Heal Me
Rafe Nauen - Family Constellations – Unravelling the Mystery of your ancestral Timeline
Stephan Hausner – Even if it costs me my life
Nadine Burke Harris - The Deepest Well
John Bradshaw - Healing the shame that binds us

Websites
https://acestoohigh.com/got-your-ace-score/
https://www.ncbi.nlm.nih.gov/pmc/articles/PMC3679131/
https://www.ted.com/talks/nadine_burke_harris_how_childhood_trauma_affects_health_across_a_lifetime
http://whatisepigenetics.com
http://www.lotusholistic.com
http://limbicreflexology.co.uk
http://neuroplastix.com/
https://rafenauen.com
https://rafesworkshops.com
https://www.acesconnection.com

About the Author

Rafe Nauen was born in 1950 in Orpington Kent. He is married to Julie Bowman and has 8 children and 14 grandchildren. He works in Derby as a constellation facilitator to private and business customers. The workshops and one to one sessions are places where people can find out quite a bit more about who they really are.

Printed in Great
Britain
by Amazon

31830713R00031